Hood Love 2

The Streets Still
Ain't Loyal

Danielle Bigsby

ISBN-13: 9780692732199

ISBN-10: 0692732195

Copyright © 2016 by Danielle Bigsby & Royal4PublishingPresents

Special discounts are available on quantity purchases by corporations, associations, and others as determined by Royal4PublishingPresents. Orders may also be shipped to be penal and correctional facilities.

Merchandise Available at:

Royal4PublishingPresents@gmail.com

Queencitybullies.com

Amazon

Urban Moon (Chesapeake, VA)

Maleah Solange (Indianapolis, IN)

Urban Read (Miami, FL)

Coming Soon to Charlotte, NC

HOOD LOVE 2: THE STREETS STILL AIN'T LOYAL

BY:

DANIELLE BIGSBY

Acknowledgements

I first want to thank God for blessing me with the talent of expressing myself with words. I want to also thank Him for implanting the vision of conveying a message through my gift that He has blessed me with. Without Him, I wouldn't exist and none of this would be possible. I want thank my children: Eniyah, Te'Ontez, Danterryia, & Da'Nae for always pushing me and motivating me to constantly become better and grow. I would also like to thank my entire support team for not allowing me to stop and give up when things looked rough. I love you and I truly thank you all from the bottom of my heart. Finally, I want to thank my fans, my Royalties & Rawyalties for taking the time out to read my books and give me feedback. I will never take that for granted. You are my inspiration and motivation to

• • •

continue doing what I love to do. I truly thank you and I love as well as appreciate you royally.

Dedication

This one is dedicated to all the victims and families who have suffered the loss of a loved one due to gun violence.

This one is for the friends of the victims who now have to ponder over the memories and cherish the bonds that they once shared.

This one is for the children who now have to grow up without a mother or father because gun violence has ripped them out of their lives.

And finally, this one is for the youth who feel pressured to become a part of the streets because they feel that no one understands them.

I only have one request:

Please put down the guns and just LIVE!!! Your life is way too valuable and the streets will only rob you of it.

Table of Contents

Tired

Are you tired?

Tired of crying?

Tired of witnessing crime scenes?

Tired of hearing gun shots?

Are you tired yet?

Tired of our youth not even seeing the age of eighteen?

Tired of having to watch mothers cry and lose their

composure while standing over their child in a casket?

Tired of losing our current generation of youth because

no one from the generations before them are willing to

take a stand?

Still not tired yet?

Tired of our babies perishing?

Tired of having to attend another funeral of a life ended

so tragically and way too soon?

Tired of explaining to our children that their friend

won't be coming back?

Hopefully,

You're finally tired.

Tired of sitting back and casually existing,

Tired of sitting around and doing nothing,

Tired of ignoring this heavy burden.

By now,

You should be tired,

Tired enough to take a stand.

Tired enough to join the movement.

Tired enough to encourage our youth,

Encourage them to put down the guns and just live.

Tired enough to realize that you have power.

Tired enough to realize that even though you are only

person,

United,

We are one voice,

And together,

We can save our babies.

Chapter 1: Too Close to Home

"That'll never happen to me."

"My homies gone ride for me."

"I stay strapped so I don't have to worry about that."

These are all lies that the streets want you to believe

because it helps to promote their agenda, but the

streets can only get you one of these two things:

REST IN PEACE

A Praying Mother

I pray they take this pain away,

But they can't.

They took a piece of my heart,

They took it away from me,

And things will never be the same.

I pray these tears stop,

But they can't.

Because the cause of my tears was one of my worst

fears,

The fear of losing the only thing that truly loved me.

I pray for peace,

But how can my mind ever really be at ease?

When it can never release the anger,

Or relinquish the torment that it was put through when

that fatal bullet pierced you.

I pray for patience,

Patience,

Patience to hold me until I'm granted answers,

Patience to guide me until I can understand why they

had to take you,

Patience to endure this pain that I have to endure life

long,

Because no part of me can be complete,

Because the one part of me that was complete,

Now no longer beats,

And my heart is forced to beat a lonely beat.

A mother prays,

That she never has to face these days,

But in this unrelenting craze,

Gun violence has taken so many of our babies away,

And I just pray,

That God somehow helps me to endure another day.

Dedicated to:

All the mothers who have had to bury their child due

to senseless gun violence

The Grief of a Family

They can never understand,

The hurt,

The pain,

The tears,

The heartfelt sorrow,

The nightmares,

The torture,

They can never truly understand.

They only celebrate you once a year,

Nine times out of ten,

It's probably your birthdate.

But as for your family,

Your face never fades away,

Family functions are never the same,

You can never sit around and laugh and cheer,

Because somewhere along the way,

Comes the tears.

The tears of having to endure the fact that you're not

here,

The pain of having to watch everyone laugh and play,

But knowing that you were the jokester of the family,

The one that actually made our day.

We can never explain our pain,

And there are just not enough words in the dictionary to

spell out our hurt,

But we have to go on,

And we have to continue,

Yet some days are worse than others,

And oh God,

We can't begin to detail the sketches of pain worn by

your mother.

Not being able to hold her child,

Or talk to her baby,

Or just say,

I love you.

We can never describe what it's like,

To walk inside her shoes.

And your little brothers and sisters,

We can't talk to them,

We don't know how to address the fact that big brother

is no longer here to protect them.

We can't explain that one single bullet ended your life,

We can't explain that this can never be made right.

We can't explain the torture of having to endure a trial,

Or for some of us,

Sitting here still not having answers,

After a very long while.

We can't explain how bad it hurts,

To look at other teenagers your age,

And know that you didn't get to live your full life,

Because someone,

A coward,

Thought it was alright,

To pull that trigger,

And end your life.

No one can endure the visions that we endure on a

constant basis,

Both day and night.

Watching your little brother grow colder by the minute,

Watching your mother cry day in and day out,

Watching your grandmother pray for strength day after

day,

Watching your dad battle internally to not seek street

justice,

The whole scene is so traumatic and sad.

And the worst part of it all is that the hood seems to find

the idea of dying cool,

Until it happens to them or someone close to their

family.

Then they want everyone to feel for them,

And express the same sentiments that our family is

feeling now.

But how can we feel some type of sadness, sympathy, or

feeling of remorse?

When they were the ones who chose to end a life so

cowardly out here in the streets,

Yet now they want us to be empathetic to their grief.

No,

They can't be serious,

This can't be real,

Because honestly speaking,

We really don't give a damn how they feel!

And we know that it's the anger from the grief cycle

speaking,

But the betrayal of someone killing our loved one,

Stings way too much.

The betrayal of knowing that someone so close to us

took our baby away,

Has murderous thoughts on our minds,

And they keep replaying repeatedly.

It all seems so wrong,

And no matter what we do,

We can't make it right.

So, we pray for peace at night,

Peace to keep on going,

Peace to endure,

Peace to calm our nerves,

Peace to be strong when we are standing in front of that

judge to hear the killer of our loved one's fate.

Peace as these torturous events play over and over again.

All that we can ask is,

"When will the grief that our family is feeling ever

end?"

Yet as of now,

That question remains without an answer.

So, we wait and pray,

And hold on to the notion that someday,

Somehow,

Some way,

We will get to see our loved one's smiling face.

Not here on Earth,

But surely in a much better place!

Why Me

Will the crying ever stop?

I see your face constantly,

I wonder what it would have been like to see you walk

across that stage,

Or what it would have been like to see you all decked

out for prom.

Constant showers of tears,

Hide my fears,

Of another one of my children dying.

Emotions bottled up,

Stuck in my throat,

Causing me to choke on my sobs,

As I hear the sounds of wailing police sirens.

Reliving the same nightmare,

The devastation of your loss is like a never-ending

movie,

Permanently etched in my mind,

Is the moment that you were carried out by six in a

casket.

Your life was over from that moment on,

And that reality to this day,

Is something that I can't seem to grasp,

No matter how hard I try.

I'm unwilling to attempt to console another mother,

Because I can't sit here and lie.

I can't tell her that it gets better with each day that

passes by,

I can't tell her that there will ever be a moment that her

eyes are dry.

Because there is no hug, card, smile or simple gesture

that can soothe this pain,

And at times,

It's very difficult to contain your rage.

You will want somebody to feel your hurt,

You will want somebody to feel your pain,

And under no circumstances,

Will you ever let your baby's death be in vain.

You see,

I smile in public,

But secretly,

This anger consumes me,

My baby's been gone for too long,

And no justice has been served.

If truth be told,

I'm ready to give up.

The pain,

The hurt,

The sadness,

The grief,

It's all too much.

I can't sleep without seeing my baby's face,

So, I try not to close my eyes.

Certain things I can't smell without tearing up,

Like their favorite perfume or cologne,

Because if it lingers for too long,

I'll be reminded of the fact that my child is never

coming back home.

I can't face life with a smile,

So, I retreat to a shell,

Feeling trapped in the middle of hell,

Figuring that death has to be better than this mental jail

cell.

I'm at the end of my rope,

I've finally lost all hope,

I no longer see the point of being here.

By my time has not yet come,

I guess God's not ready for me to die,

No matter what I try.

So, until He sees fit for me to no longer exist,

I'll have to sit back,

And wait to see what type of majestic spin he decides to

put on this.

Dedicated to:

Every parent that has lost a child due to gun violence and decided that they would rather just give up and quit...

They Will Never Know

The unimaginable pain of having to visit you through a

grave,

Can never be explained.

They can sympathize with me all they want,

But they can never truly feel my pain.

They couldn't hear the fear in that phone call,

They couldn't see that anguish at the hospital,

They couldn't visualize the agony written across my face

while standing inside the morgue.

They couldn't envision the stress of having to make

constant trips to the funeral home,

They couldn't fathom the pain hidden behind these

sunglasses,

Or the anger that the news cameras weren't able to

capture.

They can only scream out RIP,

Or put your face on a T-shirt,

Or use your death as yet another reason to get high and

drunk,

Or as an excuse to act stupid and run wild in the streets.

They can't understand what was truly lost,

They can't understand that a piece of my heart is

missing,

A piece of my foundation is gone.

They can't understand that I was robbed,

Both physically and mentally,

And they can't begin to understand how drastically my

life has changed since that day.

I can't hear my child laugh,

Or dry their tears when someone has hurt their pride.

I can't watch my child struggle to achieve their goals,

Or laugh when they hit their favorite dance move with a

little extra swag to their favorite song.

I can't brag to everyone on how they finally made it and

graduated,

Or hit them with that sideways look when they bring

home their new "Bae",

I can't help them navigate through mending broken

friendships,

Or ever be able to hear those magical words,

"Mom, you were right."

I can't watch them grow into a beautiful, responsible,

young adult;

The true depths of my hurt and pain they will never see.

The shallowness and hollowness of my heart that I carry

around with me,

They will never be privy to.

How I survive each new day,

Neither I or they will ever know.

<u>Burning Coals</u>

My heart's on fire,

My eyes burn with tears,

My mind is numb and void,

I can't put my troubled soul at ease.

Hidden traces of hurt trail down my face at night,

I have to be strong for my mom,

She can't process her hurt and pain,

When you were so carelessly murdered,

By a child lost to the streets.

Our lives changed forever in an instant,

And we are still trying to figure out why.

Girls typically cry,

But I want to fight.

I need to inflict the pain that was placed on me from this

wound,

You see,

When my daddy was stolen from me,

My life was doomed.

My little sister runs away from sadness,

She won't even mention our daddy's name.

She can't bear to even glimpse at his pictures,

Because the void and emptiness left is too strong to bear.

When mama tries to show her things from her and

daddy's younger days,

Her eyes well up,

And the tears begin to flood down,

As her emotions cascade down her face,

And the pressure of this heavy burden finally starts to

escape.

We both need our daddy,

But I need him the most,

Because it's his face that I see when I look at my

reflection in the mirror.

My face is always replaced,

And he's always there staring back at me,

Yet not able to speak.

My anger finds a way to break free,

And I find myself asking him,

"Why are you not here with me?"

"Why did you allow them to take you from me?"

"Why didn't you fight back?"

"Why won't this pain in my chest stop?"

"Why couldn't you just hold on?"

But I never get a response,

• • •

So, I continue to harbor my anger and resentment inside,

And until I see my daddy again,

Everybody is going to feel my wrath.

They will never understand,

How it feels to be in my shoes.

They will never be able to relate to how it feels to grow

up without you.

If I could only say one thing,

I know that this much is true,

I have been lost,

Since the day that I lost you…

Dedicated to:

The daughter struggling with the loss of her father

due to senseless gun violence…

Cost Me it All

This can't be reality,

You can't be gone.

We just talked last night,

You said that you were coming back home.

You said that you were just hanging out with some

friends,

Going to meet some girls,

And maybe go out on a date,

And you were just going to stay the night over there

because you knew that by the time you made it back it

would be really late.

I never once questioned the idea,

I knew these guys very well,

I trusted that you were safe with them,

I knew that they would protect you from any danger or

harm.

And now,

I'm sitting here kicking myself,

Beating myself up for being way too trusting.

I should have saw the signs of jealousy,

I should have spotted the envy in their hearts,

I should have seen them plotting from the start.

And I knew nothing about those girls,

I should have asked more questions,

But you seemed so happy.

You were beyond excited to be having such a good time,

And I didn't want to be labeled as the overbearing mom.

This time,

I didn't want to stand in the way of you having fun.

And now,

I'm full of regret on today.

You're gone,

And never coming back,

And this guilt,

I will live with,

For the rest of my life.

Wishing that I could go back in time,

And change the events of that awful, dreadful night.

The one time that I let down my guard,

It cost me,

And it cost me big.

I never thought that I would end up living life like this,

One irresponsible mistake,

Cost me you,

If only I had taken the time to investigate,

But now I can't,

Because it's too late.

In Honor of:

The Parent Battling with guilt due to the senseless

murder of their child because of gun violence...

Chapter 2: Visualize My Pain

"There is now a permanent void in our lives. We often lie awake at night and cry our hearts out. Some days, we are overjoyed by your joyous memories while on other days, we are burdened with sorrow from your loss. We have no idea why God seemed to need you so early and while we don't agree with His decision, we grudgingly accept that His will had to be done. So we pray every day for continued strength and endurance power. We constantly look to the Heavens in hopes that you, our newest Guardian Angel will watch over us from above. And all that we ask from others is to understand that we are hurting and sympathize with us. Our one constant reminder to others of how this feels is:

"Imagine how you would feel if this was you in this situation..."

Distorted Picture

They call me Black,

Yet some get the wrong idea,

Some have it twisted,

See,

I only lived what I knew.

The streets were never my main focus,

I only aimed to be a man,

I only desired to be understood,

I only wanted to be a provider,

I only needed to feel loved.

A thug I have never been,

But society sure painted me as such,

But the only question I had,

"What if I was?"

Does that mean that I deserved to die?

Does that make someone taking my life right?

Yes,

I may have been what some would have labeled as a

grown ass man,

But there were still some things that I was never taught,

Some things that I just didn't know.

The world would never get to see that I had seen the

errors of my ways,

And was slowly beginning to change.

I was starting to make that transition,

To becoming a better man.

They would never know that I had owned up to my

mistakes,

They would never see that I had started to set my

crooked path straight.

They would never see my life altering change,

Because a gun took me away.

A bullet robbed them of this vision,

A bullet robbed me of the decision,

The decision to show others that one can change.

A bullet fast forwarded my life to its' end,

And now I lie in this cold, lonely grave;

Wishing that I had the opportunity to press rewind,

And start my life all over again.

A Victim's Reflection

I didn't belong in the streets,

I didn't belong dead in the gutter,

I didn't belong in the graveyard,

I just didn't belong.

I thought that I knew it all,

I thought that I could survive,

I thought that I would be that one child that made it out

alive.

I thought that I could test the waters,

I thought that I could see what else was out there,

But that concept of testing those waters,

No longer has me here.

I didn't belong to a gang,

I just hung with that crowd,

And I didn't mean to do any of those crimes,

I was just simply hanging out.

I didn't mean to hurt anybody,

I never knew that it just might come back on me.

I didn't mean to make my mother cry,

I was just trying to do me.

I didn't mean to leave my brothers and sisters without a

role model,

I was just trying to party,

And have a little fun.

See,

I thought that my life would last forever,

I never knew that mine would end as the result of a gun.

I was young,

I was naive,

I was just imitating what I saw,

I never knew that it would end up costing me it all.

See,

I didn't mean for it to end up like this,

And I never imagined that I would have to tell you this,

From inside a cold, damp hole in the ground.

But even in death,

I have to be brave,

And allow a message to come forth through me,

A message especially designed for you.

You might be looking around and asking,

"Who?"

And to that I say,

This message is especially created for the youth.

● ● ●

I want you to know,

That you can make it out,

You can change.

I know that many people are telling you that you can't,

And that you're just going to be another statistic,

Or that you are just another product of the environment

around you,

But I promise you this,

You can survive!

Somebody should have told me that I could have made

it,

Or that I could have been something in life,

Or that I could have survived,

But they didn't.

And now it's too late for me,

But it's ok I guess,

Well really it's not,

Because this fateful turn of events could have possibly

been stopped,

If someone had just taken a stand.

But I can't blame them,

For the choices that I made.

The only thing that I can do,

Is warn you.

Before you end up in a cold, lonesome grave;

Just like me…

Dedicated to:

All the troubled youth…Both living and deceased

If I Could

My spirit looks out upon the world,

Thinking of all the things that I could have done

differently,

Wishing that I could go back in time,

And somehow make this right.

I knew deep down that the lifestyle that I was living

would only end up causing me pain,

But I thought that I had enough time left to eventually

change.

Running with that crowd,

Made the dudes on the block proud,

My actions were defining my character out loud.

But if I could have really expressed how I felt on the

inside,

My mother would have broken down and cried.

I only hit the block in search of what I didn't have,

I was trying to find what my life was lacking,

I was looking for the only thing that would have made

my life complete,

I needed a father figure,

I desired a male role model,

To fill the void in my life.

So, the dudes on the block gave me something to look up

to,

They had the money,

They had the girls,

They had the cars,

They had the fame,

They had the respect,

Everything that I thought a man should have in his

possession.

See,

While my age labeled me as a boy,

My character,

My demeanor,

My wisdom,

And my mentality,

Defined me as a man according to the streets.

Plus,

I had to do something to fill the void left in our home,

I had to fill the shoes that were left abandoned by the

man who was supposed to teach me everything,

The man who was supposed to prepare me for this cold,

cruel world.

But I wasn't equipped for what lay ahead,

And didn't know exactly what I was really getting into,

And that is why,

My voice is now speaking from my final resting place to

you.

If only I could go back and rethink my decisions,

I would change my ways,

Because my mother now cries every single day.

And my soul will forever have to bear the knowledge of

knowing that I am the cause,

I was trying to grow up too fast,

And that one unwise decision ended up sealing my fate.

If only I could turn back the hands of time...

• • •

Be Strong

I have done so much,

Yet I have done so little.

My life was just beginning,

Even though some of my goals in life did get

accomplished.

I graduated from high school,

I made my mom so proud when I walked across the

stage.

But neither one of us could have imagined,

Neither would we have ever seen this coming,

My death,

My untimely demise,

It came way too soon.

The shrieking heard from her screams and cries,

Was oh so painful and loud.

• • •

I was a good kid,

Sure, I messed up from time to time,

But I was just beginning to live life,

I was simply trying to find out exactly who this person

was that lived deep within my mind.

Honestly,

I thought that I had so much more time.

My mother was the closest thing to perfection that I had,

And as I watch from Heaven,

I can see that her heart is hurt so bad.

A foolish person took away the best thing that she had,

The one thing so precious,

The one thing that they can't give back,

My life.

So,

I sit and wait,

My soul in lingo,

Awaiting her,

Waiting until we're reunited,

So, that she can once again be glad.

I hope that she knows,

I do see everything.

And as I observe her,

I sit back and smile.

I watch her success,

That's my mom,

And I'm so proud!!!

So please don't look at the bad in this situation,

Because I no longer have to face nor deal with this cold

and unrelenting world,

I'm finally free.

So, continue to live,

And be as happy as can be,

For you only lost me physically…

Dedicated in Jory Sweatt's honor to his mother:

Kendra Reeves

Feel My Sorrow

I grieved the moment that I got the news,

I grieved the moment that I had to verify that the body

that was actually lying there was you;

I grieved the moment that my worst nightmare actually

came true.

The tears fell immediately,

The deafening screams were brought to fruition and

given life,

In that horrific night.

Mourning you,

Every single day,

Wanting to exchange my life for yours,

If this was only possible in some type of way.

Putting on a smile,

To hide and shield the pain,

But on the inside,

My soul is drained.

No more fight left in me,

I really just want to quit,

Joining my child in death,

Is a thought that on a daily basis,

I fight hard to resist.

Refusing to look at your pictures,

Because the burden is too big to bear.

They say that God heals all wounds,

But sometimes I question if He is really there.

I know that I am talking nonsense,

But I'm speaking from a real place of hurt and pain,

Maybe I could rejoice,

Or at least be ok,

If I was able to see your face again.

So, bear with me,

If you see me shedding a tear,

Hold me tight.

If I let out an unrelenting scream,

I just ask that you weather the storm with me,

No matter how difficult I appear to be,

Or how hard this journey may seem.

Feel my sorrow,

And be empathetic as well as sympathetic,

And don't push me away,

Don't make me feel isolated,

Don't make me feel rejected,

Especially now,

When I really need you the most…

Dedicated to:

All parents and guardians who have lost a child to

gun violence

A Load to Carry

Imagine having to go on,

Without someone that you love.

One fatal decision,

Shattered your reality.

Visualize having to tell your loved ones,

That their loved one won't be coming home tonight,

Because fatal bullets,

Robbed them of their life.

Envision having to plan a funeral,

Instead of a birthday celebration,

Or a graduation party.

Having to shed tears of mourning,

When I should have been celebrating, you embarking

into adulthood.

Could you even fathom,

The size of the burden that I have to carry on a

consistent basis?

The number of tears that my pillow has had to hold,

The sadness hidden behind my eyes,

The void that lives within my soul?

The hurt of losing a vital piece of me weighs me down,

But how do I let go?

To let go,

Means to forget about you,

And I refuse to do as such.

Losing you has altered my life way too much…

Dedicated to:

Everyone who has lost a loved one due to gun

violence

<u>Inflicted Wounds</u>

My soul is stained,

My heart is tarnished,

My mind bleeds of pain.

My face is flooded,

My feet walk on eggshells,

My ears ring with screams.

My dreams are now nightmares,

Vivid hauntings of that day leave me scared.

My cries relinquish the emptiness of my soul,

From you no longer being here with me,

Echoing from a place of genuine hurt.

The wounds inflicted to my child that fateful day were

physical,

But the anguish did not stop there,

Because the wounds inflicted on my heart,

And the sadness forever etched in my brain,

Has me questioning my sanity.

And if I will ever be able to live life,

And somehow survive this pain,

Simply because,

On that day,

My life forever changed…

The Cycle Repeats

I thought that the harshness of life without you would

finally settle after a period of grieving,

But that's not the case.

First comes the sadness,

The loss,

And the grief.

Then the heartache,

The heartbreak,

And the depression.

I'm constantly stressing,

Wishing that I could behold your face just one more

time.

Next,

Reality sets in,

And I realize that I have no choice other than to move on

without you.

Although I battle with accepting this new life,

I have no other option.

So, I take it day by day,

And slowly begin to settle into a routine,

I carry you with me,

Everywhere that I go,

Because no matter what anyone else says,

I refuse to let you go.

But when years start to pile up and I have no answers,

The cycle begins again,

Starting all over with anger.

I'm mad because my child's killer is still roaming free,

I'm mad because justice hasn't been served for my child

or me.

I'm mad because the streets are holding on to this "No

Snitching" Code,

Knowing that somebody out there knows.

I'm mad because my baby has been forgotten,

And I am the only one who has been making sure that

their memory carries on,

While fighting both day and night to stay strong.

Then,

I'm sad because my heart is filled with emptiness.

Yet,

I somehow push forward,

Constantly and consistently praying to God for strength

and endurance.

For the worst part, has not even started,

The day that I have to sit there,

And stare my child's killer in the face,

Will be one of my most trying times.

Anger,

Sadness,

Resentment,

Hurt,

Rage,

And vengeance,

Will rise to the surface,

As I battle with myself to sit and endure the

antagonizing pain of my baby's trial.

Knowing that I have to somehow contain myself,

And keep my emotions in check,

In order for my child to receive justice.

But it's so hard,

I'm an emotional wreck,

My feelings are all over the place,

And this grief cycle begins repeating itself once again.

I need God to hold me,

I need God to bring my constant sobs to an end.

I am begging God to help me with this scream that is

lodged deep within my throat,

Threatening to force its' way out.

Witnessing the evidence as it is paraded about in the

courtroom,

Crime scene photos are forcing me to vividly remember

that day,

Yet again,

My heart breaks.

And as this emotional roller-coaster continues,

I begin to realize one thing,

This cycle of grief,

From losing my child will only repeat over and over

again,

This emotional tidal wave of life without my child will

never end.

Chapter 3: See Gun Violence

Through Us

"The epidemic is never as effective if you don't put a

face with it. So, in this next section, there will be

pictures enclosed to be sure that you will always

remember what the faces of gun violence look like.

Their deaths will not be in vain!!!"

I am the face of gun violence…

I am Ronquez "Quez" Bigsby

Birth Date: October 16, 1995

Death Date: August 11, 2010

Age in 2010 at time of death: 14

Birthday that would have been celebrated in 2016: 21

Your Memory Lives On!!!

I am the face of gun violence...

I am Cheryl Phillips

Birth Date: April 28, 1968

Death Date: May 23, 2006

Age in 2006 at time of death: 38

Birthday that would have been celebrated in 2016: 48

Children left to cherish memory: 1

Your Memory Lives On!!!

I am the face of gun violence...

I am Antonio "Tony" Kelly

Birth Date: March 24, 1991

Death Date: February 28, 2011

Age in 2011 at time of death: 20

Birthday that would have been celebrated in 2016: 26

Children left to cherish memory: 3

Your Memory Lives On!!!

I am the face of gun violence...

I am Tyrone Reece

Birth Date: May 9, 1983

Death Date: June 21, 2013

Age in 2013 at time of death: 30

Birthday that would have been celebrated in 2016: 33

Children left to cherish his memory: 2

Your Memory Lives On!!!

I am the face of gun violence…

I am Anton "Juve" Irvin

Birth Date: March 27, 1985

Death Date: March 28, 2008

Age in 2008 at time of death: 23

Birthday that would have been celebrated in 2016: 31

Your Memory Lives On!!!

I am the face of gun violence…

I am Lamar "MoneyMar" Hughes

Birth Date: December 6, 1993

Death Date: September 5, 2010

Age in 2010 at time of death: 16

Birthday that would have been celebrated in 2016: 23

Your Memory Lives On!!!

I am the face of gun violence…

I am Keith "Big Ke" Battle

Birth Date: December 9, 1981

Death Date: June 16, 2015

Age in 2015 at time of death: 33

Birthday that would have been celebrated in 2016: 35

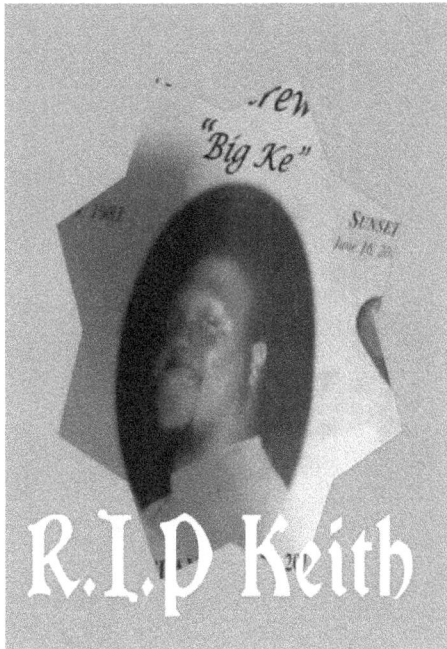

Your Memory Lives On!!!

I am the face of gun violence...

I am Jory Sweatt

Birth Date: December 3, 1995

Death Date: October 22, 2015

Age in 2015 at time of death: 19

Birthday that would have been celebrated in 2016: 21

Your Memory Lives On!!!

I am the face of gun violence…

I am Row'Neisha "Weba" Overton

Birth Date: June 16, 1999

Death Date: May 26, 2015

Age in 2015 at time of death: 15

Birthday that would have been celebrated in 2016: 17

Your Memory Lives On!!!

I am the face of gun violence...

I am Issac "I Ball" Hutcherson

Birth Date: January 18, 1977

Death Date: June 29, 2005

Age in 2005 at time of death: 28

Birthday that would have been celebrated in 2016: 39

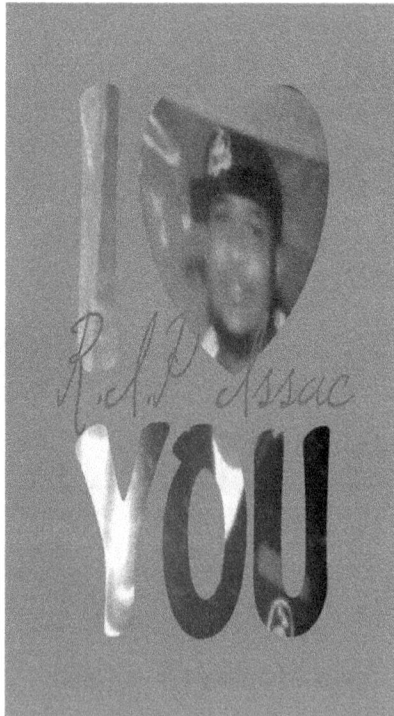

Your Memory Lives On!!!

I am the face of gun violence...

I am Antoine Meeks

Birth Date: October 20, 1984

Death Date: December 1, 2003

Age in 2003 at time of death: 19

Birthday that would have been celebrated in 2016: 32

Children left to cherish memory: 1

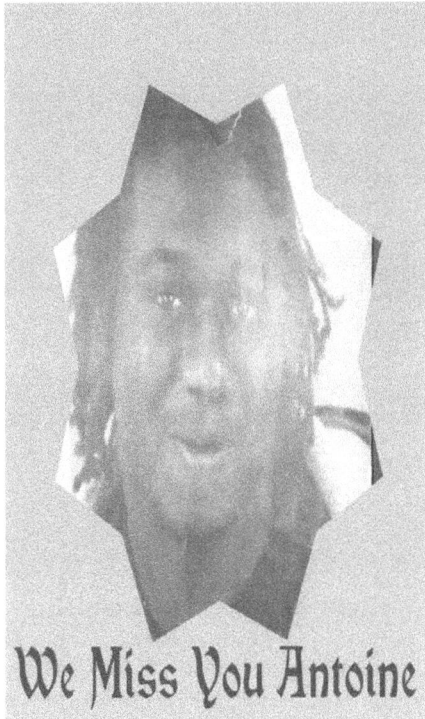

We Miss You Antoine

Your Memory Lives On!!!

I am the face of gun violence…

I am John "Black" Sykes

Birth Date: December 19, 1981

Death Date: April 29, 2015

Age in 2015 at time of death: 33

Birthday that would have been celebrated in 2016: 35

Children left to cherish memory: 7

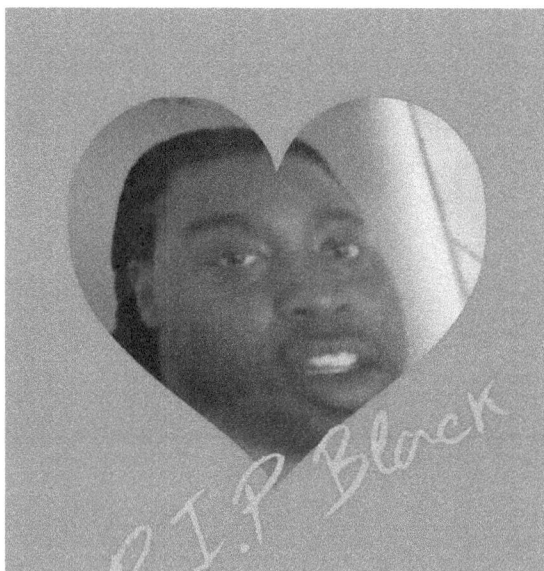

Your Memory Lives On!!!

Chapter 4: Look Through the

Lenses

"The hardest part of any journey is self-discovery. It
is even more unfortunate when you don't discover
what could have saved you from tragedy and
heartache until it's too late. So, as we lay cold,
lifeless, and still in our graves, our souls are left in
lingo trying to figure out what we could have done to
spare our loved ones from this current grief that they
are currently having to endure. Regret consumes jus
and we just wish that we could somehow turn back
the hands of time. Although the latter is not possible,
we can still make a difference. We can use our voices
through the words shared on these pages of the Hood
Love series to help steer another individual from the
path that we chose. We can share our stories to shield

another family from this burden of pain and sorrow.

We can step up to the plate and save another child

before it's too late. Although our lives are now over,

the next generation of lives doesn't have to be."

<u>My Own Worst Enemy</u>

Reflecting back on my life has me mad at myself,

You see,

The only reason that I lay cold in this hole in the ground,

Is because of choices that I made.

I was living the life of a real savage,

Enjoying the thrill of wreaking havoc on anyone in sight,

Because I had nothing better to do with my life.

I robbed many parents of their children and never even

thought twice about it,

I stole anything that I could get my hands on,

And intentionally poisoned my entire community with

drugs,

I didn't have a care in the world,

Because I was simply having fun.

• • •

I never even stopped to think of the consequences of my

actions,

You see,

I wasn't the only one out there in the streets that was

packing a burner.

But I must have pulled the trigger one too many times,

Because the next life that would be taken would

ultimately wind up being mine.

Somebody's homie,

Somebody's father,

Somebody's mother,

Somebody's sister,

Somebody's aunt,

Somebody's uncle,

Somebody's cousin,

Somebody's brother,

Somebody's niece,

Somebody's nephew,

Somebody's child,

Refused to allow my indiscretions in the street a chance

to slide.

Somebody's loved one,

Just wouldn't let bygones be bygones,

They just wouldn't let it ride.

Somebody's best friend decided to take action,

They all came together,

And decided that it was now my time to die.

It's just too bad that I didn't realize,

That I was the only person who had the power to make it

right.

I didn't capitalize on the chance,

To make something out of my life,

I had become my own worst enemy,

And it inevitably ended up costing me my life.

Now as I lay here and reflect from this grave,

Desiring so badly to make it right,

I must suck it up and face my reality,

And continuously pray that my tragic occurrence can

somehow affect someone else.

Pray that my downfall and demise come together and

paint a realistic picture of how conniving the streets can

be,

Pray that through my story,

I can discourage a young child from that lifestyle,

And with God's grace,

Save a life.

Piece Be Still

I can't express exactly what I felt deep down inside

when I felt the power and coldness of the steel from that

commanding piece beneath my fingertips,

But I do know that it is one that I will never forget.

In a sense,

It was feeling that can only be described as irreplaceable.

Yet in a totally different sense,

It had me feeling like a coward because I only felt

powerful when I had my piece in my hands.

No one could ever touch me,

Or at least that's what I thought,

As I held on firmly and tightly to my gun.

But hiding behind my gun,

Refusing to get down in the mud and fight,

Or as my generation likes to say,

Refusing to throw them hands,

Had me labeled as scary and weak.

But as long as I had my gun,

They would never venture out to speak their minds,

And their opinions were never voiced out loud.

They were always too afraid that one ill spoken word

against me to the wrong person,

Would cause my trigger finger to itch.

So, with so much distrust in my heart,

I would never be found around town without my peace

maker.

I ate with it,

I clubbed with it,

I got drunk with it,

I got high with it,

I even took a shit with it.

The only time that we ever separated was when I took a

shower,

But you bet your bottom dollar,

That it was definitely within arm's reach.

It provided so much power,

That I let it spark carelessly,

Causing chaos in the streets,

Yet my burner seemed to settle any beef.

But the whole time that I was bragging out there in the

streets,

I never stopped to analyze the fact that there could have

been somebody out there bigger and harder than me.

See,

This next generation of youth is far more advanced and

always eager to put in work,

They are harder the generations before them,

And I had been sleeping and not even paying attention,

And that oversight would quickly have my time coming

to an end,

But I refused to take heed.

While creating confusion in the streets,

I pissed off quite a few people,

And made some enemies out in the hood.

But believing that my piece would make them stand

down and be still,

I carelessly ignored the noise that they were talking.

They were moving in silence,

While I was barking out loud.

And one night while I was a little too intoxicated,

My life went up in a cloud of smoke.

A hailstorm of bullets tore my body into shreds,

Creating holes resembling those that are found in Swiss

Cheese.

Life as I knew it,

Was now over,

I had become another fallen victim of the streets.

The piece that I had relied on to keep others still,

Had finally come,

And in the blink of an eye,

Had just silenced me.

Worth

I wanted to relieve my mom of her stress,

Needed to lift the burden of daddy walking out on us,

So, I headed to the one place where I saw easy money

being made,

And I knew that a street hustle would save the day.

But in order to survive the streets,

I had to be able to protect myself,

And although I didn't want to,

I knew that getting a gun was my only option for safety.

See,

When getting money,

The haters emerge like cockroaches do when they smell

food after the lights have gone out,

With a plot to rob you,

Because they are too lazy to get a hustle of their own.

So, if push came to shove,

I would have to pull that trigger.

To keep my mom from struggling,

I would kill Satan himself with my bare hands.

The money started to flow,

And finally,

We were beginning to live good.

And although my mom didn't like the idea,

As well as being against me being involved in this type

of lifestyle,

She welcomed the uplifting of some of the pressure off

her shoulders.

You see,

Taking care of multiple children on her own with no

help at all,

Had broken her spirit down,

And her life was a little less hectic without all the piled

up overdue bills scrolled across the house.

With her son's help,

She was finally able to give her kids some of the finer

things in life.

But what goes up,

Must always come back down,

And all good things ultimately come to an end.

His reign on the streets,

Came to a screeching halt,

One dreadful night,

When some coward took his life.

• • •

He only wanted to make life easier for his family,

A true testament to his character as a man,

But the Grim Reaper stripped him of his life,

Before he was fully able to implement his plan.

And now,

His mother is left to question,

"Was it all worth it?"

Dedicated to:

The young men killed by guns who had to fill the void

and shoes left behind by the men who abandoned

their responsibilities...

<u>Too Late</u>

Ever wanted to say "I'm sorry",

But you couldn't?

Ever wanted to start all over,

But couldn't rewind the hands of time?

Ever wanted to erase a mistake,

But time revealed that it was too late?

Ever wanted to begin again with a clean slate,

But realized from this type of trance your body couldn't

seem to awaken?

Ever wished that you could just look down at your child

once more,

Just to adore their smile?

Ever reminisced on just how proud you would have

made your parents,

If only more time on Earth had been allowed?

Ever saturated your pillow with tears from a moment

engraved permanently in your mind,

A moment where time actually stood still?

Ever wanted to change your life but you lay cold in an

empty grave?

Ever longed to be a better parent,

But couldn't because death has taken your baby away?

Ever wished that somebody could relate to your pain?

Ever wished that you didn't feel like your loved meant

nothing to others beside you?

Ever wished that your tragedy could change somebody's

life?

Well,

You can!

Share your story,

Although it hurts.

Reveal your pain,

Your tears can turn someone's footsteps…

Create triumph from tragedy,

Because it's never too late to make a difference!!!

·

Time Doesn't Stop

Can I rewind the hands of time?

This grave is so damp and cold,

And my body's not ready to depart from its' soul,

I'm fighting so hard,

But this situation is out of my control,

And now every inch of my being must endure this

permanent torture and hurt as a whole.

Recycling thoughts of when times were happier,

Remembering how I used to run around outside barefoot

with the goofiest smile on my face,

Thinking of all the times that my mom would get out

there in the backyard and wrestle with me and my

friends.

Revisiting the time when my mom watched me struggle

while trying to learn how to ride a bike,

The smile that graced her face when I finally caught on

and got it.

Thinking on all the times that she gave me her undivided

attention even though she worked constant doubles at

her job,

Or remembering all the many countless nights that she

stayed up preparing our family for the next day,

Paying special attention to every detail and making sure

that everything was just right.

And how did I repay her?

I kept her up even more nights way beyond her normal

timeframe,

Crying and wondering exactly where I was.

Praying to God to shield me from any unseen danger,

And protect me from any unknown harm.

While I never seemed to pay any attention,

It was her prayers that kept me on this Earth for so long.

But as the elders always say,

When you play with fire,

You will definitely soon get burnt.

I didn't take heed to any of the warnings,

And my mom always said,

"Warning comes before destruction!"

Thinking that I would always have time,

I continued on my path of devastation,

And left my mother's heart with a deep, gaping hole;

And an extreme void,

And her life forever destroyed.

Now,

I lie in this grave,

Wishing and hoping that I could turn back the hands of

time,

But knowing that it's not possible.

Wishing that I could dry my mother's tears,

But knowing that I can't.

Wishing that I could ease my mother's pain,

While knowing that I am the one who caused it.

Wishing that I could dull her heartache,

While knowing that I am the one who caused her heart

to break.

So, I need her to please hear my whisper from the grave,

As I say,

"I'm so sorry Mommy."

Dedicated to:

Every rebellious soul lost to the streets wishing that

they could get a second chance to make it right

<u>Dose of Reality</u>

The shadow of my footprints are deep,

The impression that they left are long lasting.

And if you place your feet inside,

You are sure to sink,

Because it is all a trap.

The path that they trailed,

Can only bring harm,

They lead to a road full of deception,

They follow a path of pure destruction and devastation,

Nothing good can come from this walk of life.

If my death has taught you nothing,

I want you to embrace this thought,

"The streets have no loyalty!"

They will surely eat you alive,

Then chew you up,

And spit you out.

So please do me and your parents this one huge favor,

Avoid the streets,

And just enjoy life.

Dedicated to:

Those streets commanders now pained with regret

from their street lifestyles

My Wish

I know that it feels like I left you in this world all alone,

But unfortunately,

God called me home.

I know it hurts because you can't see me every day,

And there was so much that we didn't get to say,

But my Father in Heaven said that I could no longer

stay.

I know that you feel that you were robbed of countless

opportunities with me,

But I need you to hold on for dear life to our memories,

And always remember,

That I still carry you with me.

We are only separated by flesh,

I have now become your angel in Heaven,

And I am now watching your every move.

I cheer for you in spirit,

Every time that you accomplish something that you

thought you couldn't do,

I catch every tear that you have ever shed,

I feel every burden that you have had to carry.

And to you I want to say,

Don't cry for me.

You see,

I don't hurt anymore,

My soul is now at peace.

Smile and enjoy life,

Because you didn't lose me,

You simply gained another Guardian Angel.

I loved you then,

And I still love you now!

So, go ahead and live your life,

Just remember to continue to do what you love,

And always know that I am proud!!!

Dedicated to:

Everyone who must continue without their loved one

Chapter 5: Play Your Part

"Everyone tends to believe that once a victim dies and has been buried, the big part is over. They tend to believe that they no longer have to be supportive or care. But the issue of gun violence is a universal one. Everyone must come together and tackle this issue head on. Take back our babies and let them know that we do care about them. Mothers, stand up and be mothers. If you don't how to be one, ask questions. There is help out there. And elders, stop judging. Use the wisdom that you have gained to help uplift the next generation. Fathers, step up and let your voices be heard. Our children need male role models back in their lives. You are a vital part of the structure within the home. Neighbors, bring back a sense of community. Get to know your neighbors and their children. Know exactly who your children are playing with and who they are hanging out with at all times. And neighbors, if you see your neighbor's child acting up or getting into trouble, please speak up! Be sure to let their parents know exactly what you did and why. It takes a village to successfully raise a child. Grandmothers, PLEASE come back!!! We need those grandmothers that would get in your tail if you even thought about acting up or showing out like you weren't raised with common sense. It's ok to have age on you because length in years of life on this Earth signifies wisdom!!! Youth, learn to fight with your minds... You are powerful beyond measure!!! We just need you to think before you act. If you unite and put your powerful minds together, you can overcome!!! With solid leadership behind you, you can make a change and a difference.

The biggest thing that we can all do is:

Build a personal relationship with God and get to

know Him for yourself. On top of that, PRAY!!!

Because prayer changes things…"

Our Responsibility

Every time another parent mourns the loss of their child,

Society has a problem.

Every time that gun violence steals away another one of

our innocent babies,

Communities should have something to say.

Each time that a child must become parentless due to

bullets,

Someone should refuse to let the media forget about it.

Each time that someone is senselessly murdered in our

streets,

Their memory should be more than a rest in peace t-

shirt.

• • •

Each time that guns rob us of yet another individual,

Their lives shouldn't only be remembered through a

candlelight vigil.

We must do better!!!

There is no easy way to fix this problem,

But unity is definitely the start.

Take back our children,

Take back our neighborhoods,

Fill our babies full of love,

And bring God back into their lives.

It won't cure the problem,

But it's definitely a step towards making it right.

There is no one person to blame,

We all have dropped the ball somewhere.

Fathers,

Help raise your daughters and sons,

Mothers can't be the only ones trying to get the job

done.

Mothers,

Let go of the anger and resentment towards your

childrens' fathers,

Our babies need their fathers as much as they need you.

Petty differences no longer matter,

When it's a matter of life and death,

Come together,

Before memories of your child are all that you have left.

The responsibility of saving our babies belongs to each

and every one of us,

So please do your best to do your part!!!

Dedicated to:

Those who want to help but don't know exactly how

they lend their assistance

Help Carry the Torch

Death is always difficult for anyone to deal with,

It causes tears,

Sadness,

Pain,

Agony,

Heartache and grief.

Now imagine the feelings of families who have endured

the loss of a loved one due to gun violence,

The impact is traumatic and twice as difficult,

And no one wants to be in their shoes.

So oftentimes,

Others feel for them,

But have no idea or concept of what they can do to help,

Or how to improve the situation for the families.

Well,

Ways to help are more convenient than one may know,

One never has to go out of their way to help.

It's really quite simple,

Just greet them with a simple smile,

Or ask them,

"How was their day?"

Say something funny to make them smile,

Because laughter is always good for the soul.

Take a stand against gun violence,

Help save someone's child,

Pick up the torch,

Help keep these victims' memories alive.

Show the world that there is a message to be heard

through these children's deaths,

Speak their names out loud,

And tell someone else,

Tell it to everyone that you come in contact with,

Until there's no one left to tell…

<u>Special Thanks</u>

Special thanks goes out to everyone who is a part of the making of this book and the stand that it takes against gun violence. I appreciate you for understanding and being willing to be a part of what it represents. Special thanks also goes to each and every one of you that have purchased this book and received the messages that have been told through these victims' unfortunate and untimely deaths. I thank you for listening to the pain through their stories and now I must ask something of you. I ask you to not allow these victims' stories and lives to be vain. I ask you to spread the message found in this book and the volumes before it as well as the volumes to come. Share this book with anyone that you come in contact with. Do your part to help save our babies…

Support the movement that has spawned from the

birth and creation of the Hood Love Series...

Hood Love: The Just Live Movement

FB: HoodLove JustLive

FB: Hood Love: The Movement@justlivemovement

Email: JustLiveTheMovement@gmail.com

Remember the face that forced life into this

movement...

Ronquez A. Bigsby

s.i.p gods angel

Follow the Hood Love Series...

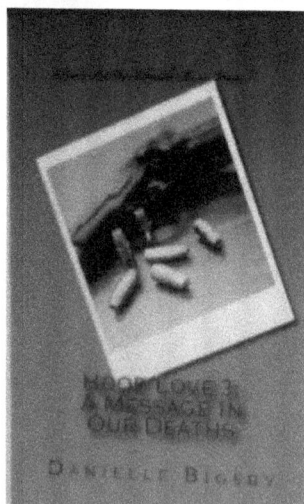

(Coming 8/11/2017)

/

www.ingramcontent.com/pod-product-compliance
Lightning Source LLC
Chambersburg PA
CBHW020912090426
42736CB00008B/601